THE DIVINE CONSPIRACY

JESUS' MASTER CLASS FOR LIFE

SIX SESSIONS

with Kevin and Sherry Harney

DALLAS WILLARD

ZONDERVAN®

ZONDERVAN.com/
AUTHORTRACKER
follow your favorite authors

ZONDERVAN

The Divine Conspiracy Participant's Guide
Copyright © 2010 by Dallas Willard

Requests for information should be addressed to:

Zondervan, *Grand Rapids, Michigan 49530*

ISBN 978-0-310-32439-3

Cover and interior illustration: Charles Ryskamp
Interior design: Sherri L. Hoffman

Printed in the United States of America

HB 02.16.2023

CONTENTS

A Word from Dallas Willard 7

SESSION ONE
The Divine Conspiracy 11

SESSION TWO
The Path to a Blessed Life 25

SESSION THREE
Becoming a Good Person 37

SESSION FOUR
Treasuring What Matters Most 51

SESSION FIVE
Becoming a Community of Prayerful Love 65

SESSION SIX
Living as a Disciple of Jesus 77

A WORD FROM DALLAS WILLARD

Discipleship to Jesus is the very heart of the gospel. The really good news for humanity is that Jesus is now taking students in the master class of life. The eternal life that begins with confidence in Jesus is a life in his present kingdom, now on earth and available to all. So the message of and about him is specifically a gospel for our life now, not just for dying. It is about living now as his apprentice in kingdom living, not just as a consumer of his merits. Our future, however far we look, is a natural extension of the faith by which we live now and the life in which we now participate. Eternity is now in flight and we with it, like it or not.

It is my hope, in these six sessions, to provide an understanding of the gospel that will open the way for the people of Christ actually to do — do once again, for they have done it in the past — what their acknowledged Maestro said to do. Perhaps the day will come when the "Great Commission" of Matthew 28:18 – 20 would be fully and routinely implemented as the objective, the "mission statement," of the Christian churches, one by one and collectively.

Individual Christians still hear Jesus say, "Whoever hears these words of mine and does them is like those intelligent people who build their houses upon rock," standing firm against every pressure of life (Matthew 7:24 – 25, my paraphrase). How life-giving it would be if their understanding of the gospel allowed them simply to reply, "I will do them! I will find out how. I will devote my life to it! This is the best life strategy I ever heard of!" and then go off to their fellowship and its teachers, and into their daily life, to learn how to live in his kingdom as Jesus indicated was best.

Dallas Willard

OF NOTE

The quotations interspersed throughout this participant's guide are excerpts from the book *The Divine Conspiracy* by Dallas Willard (HarperOne, 1997) as well as pieces from material gathered during the shooting of this DVD curriculum.

THE DIVINE CONSPIRACY

God is at work doing something very big in this world ...
but it often goes unnoticed. We get glimpses of this "Divine
Conspiracy" and hear the whisper of Jesus inviting us to enter
in. The choice is up to us.

INTRODUCTION

The divine conspiracy is breaking into human history. It comes not with an eardrum-splitting crash, but as a gentle whisper. The message is simple, but absolutely life changing. God's kingdom is not just coming ... it is here, in our midst. If we listen closely and follow the invitation to be part of this work of God in the world, our lives will never be the same.

There are signs and indicators that the divine conspiracy is at work in our midst and that we are entering into it.

God longs to entrust his presence and power in the lives of ordinary human beings. To do this, he must grow character within us and often this is forged in the fires of adversity, pain, and loss. Is God growing your character through the tough times of life? The kingdom is near!

The gospel is more than an offer of cleansing from personal sin or a battle against injustice in this world. It is about the way we live life today. Grace not only cleanses us, but it is the fuel that propels us forward as we bring the presence and love of God into the world each day. As we live for Jesus and bring his love to the world, the kingdom is near.

God is more aware of the pain in this world than we are. Yet, he is a God of joy and overflows with happiness. When his joy is in us and we let it resonate wherever we go, the kingdom of God is near.

"Repent, for the kingdom of the heavens is at hand" (Matt. 3:2; 4:17; 10:7). This is a call for us to reconsider how we have been approaching our life, in light of the fact that we now, in the presence of Jesus, have the option of living within the surrounding movements of God's eternal purposes, of taking our life into his life.

TALK ABOUT IT

Jesus calls himself our "Friend," but he is also our teacher (Rabbi). Tell about one way Jesus has become your teacher and how you are growing as his student. What practical things can we include in a normal day that help us become a more teachable student of Jesus?

To trust the real person Jesus is to have confidence in him in every dimension of our real life, to believe that he is right about and adequate to everything.

VIDEO TEACHING NOTES

As you watch the video teaching segment for session one, featuring John Ortberg's conversation with Dallas Willard, use the following outline to record anything that stands out to you.

The meaning of "divine conspiracy"

The importance of character

Understanding "the gospel"

God is present with human beings now

Becoming a student or apprentice of Jesus Christ

The good news of Jesus contrasted to the gospel of sin management

A fresh understanding of grace

God as Father

The happiness of God

In the Gospels, "the gospel" is the good news of the presence and availability of life in the kingdom, now and forever, through reliance on Jesus the Anointed.

VIDEO DISCUSSION

1. What is an example of something God is doing in the world, but many people don't notice or realize it?

2. Dallas Willard believes that God might allow hard things in this life so that he can develop character in his children. How have you seen life's tough times and painful circumstances grow character in yourself or in others and draw you/them closer to Jesus?

3. Willard suggests that God wants to develop character in people so that he can trust them with his power. What are some possible consequences when a person has power but does not have character shaped by God?

4. **Read:** Matthew 6:25–34. What does it mean to "seek first his kingdom"? When you are really seeking God's kingdom first, what kinds of attitudes and actions rise to the surface in your life?

God's own "kingdom," or "rule," is the range of his effective will, where what he wants done is done.

---

5. Willard says that one of the keys to becoming an apprentice and student of Jesus is to "think well enough of Jesus to trust him." How can this impact how we walk through life?

6. The gospel of sin management is all about what to do with sin. For some, it is about what we do about our personal sin. For others, it is what we do about structural evils such as injustice and poverty. How have you seen both of these approaches to sin management in the lives of believers?

Another way to look at the good news of Jesus is to ask not only the question, "What do we do about sin?" but "What do we do about life?" How might our approach to Jesus and the gospel be transformed if we spent more time asking the latter?

History has brought us to the point where the Christian message is thought to be essentially concerned only with how to deal with sin: with wrongdoing or wrong-being and its effects. Life, our actual existence, is not included in what is now presented as the heart of the Christian message, or it is included only marginally.

7. Willard defines grace as "God's action in our lives to help us do what we can't do on our own." When you think of grace, what comes to mind? How does Willard's explanation of grace include the forgiveness of sins, but take us even further?

8. Willard suggests the best way to think of God is as a father. How do you respond to this invitation?

In an ideal world, what should a healthy father do, and how could this mirror what God desires to do for his children?

9. **Read:** Genesis 1:29–31. What are examples of the joy and happiness of God that we see throughout the Bible?

10. What have you learned in your journey through life that helps you continue to grow in happiness even when things are painful and difficult?

BONUS STUDY

If your group has time, you may choose to watch the bonus section of the video for session one now. (If not, consider viewing it on your own or as a group as part of your between-sessions activities.) Here are some reflection questions for the bonus section:

When people ask, "Have you trusted in Jesus?" they usually mean, have you asked for Jesus to forgive your sins and have you accepted him so that you will go to heaven some day? How does this understanding of trusting Jesus take on new significance and texture when we also add the meaning: "Do you trust him enough that each day you do the things that he taught?"

How is trusting in Jesus a one-time event as well as a daily discipline?

How does the biblical understanding of "kingdom" differ from a strictly political and secular definition?

CLOSING PRAYER

Take time as a group to pray in some of the following directions:

- Thank God for his happiness and ask for him to let this same joy dwell in you and flow from you to others.
- Ask the Holy Spirit to open your ears to hear the whispers of the kingdom and the message of the divine conspiracy.
- Praise God for those moments when the beauty of his creation reminds you of his presence and activity in the world.
- Surrender your life, time, mind, and passions to God and ask him to use you in his divine conspiracy.

BETWEEN SESSIONS

Personal Reflection

St. Augustine wrote about a place inside human beings that only God can fill, a need that only Jesus can satisfy. What are some of the things people do that reveal a deep sense of emptiness in their lives? In those moments when you are not tuned into God's presence and work, what are some of the places you can end up searching that are not life-giving? How can you turn your focus more directly on God's kingdom in such moments?

Personal Action

Take a walk somewhere in creation that you naturally see God's presence. As you walk, talk with your heavenly Father. Thank him for all he has made. Imagine him looking on the beauty of this world and all the galaxies, and picture his delight. Celebrate with him. Then, remember that the pinnacle of God's creation is people, his children. Think about how God celebrates you and meditate on the reality that your life brings the Father joy and you make him happy.

Recommended Reading

As you reflect on what you have learned in this session you may want to read chapters 1–3 of the book *The Divine Conspiracy* by Dallas Willard. Then, in preparation for session two, you may want to read chapter 4 as well.

JOURNAL, REFLECTIONS, AND NOTES

THE PATH TO A BLESSED LIFE

The pathway to a blessed life is not a rigorous effort to become poor in spirit, meek, or mournful. True blessing is offered to all who are tired, weary, hurting, lonely, merciful, pure, and persecuted. The kingdom life of Jesus is offered to all who will simply receive it.

INTRODUCTION

The Sermon on the Mount is the most powerful and influential talk ever given. In it, Jesus speaks to real people and invites them to enter a whole new kind of life ... life in the kingdom of God.

There are three big questions we all ask as we seek to live and walk in this new kingdom life. (1) What is real? (2) Who is well off? (3) How can I be a really good person? When we hear the voice of Jesus speaking in the Sermon on the Mount we are quickly surprised to learn that the answers to these questions are dramatically different than we have thought.

When we learn what is real, discover how well off we are, and begin to live as really good people, Jesus' kingdom presence and power cascades from our hearts, lives, homes, and churches, and covers the earth. As this happens we become profoundly aware that when God's blessing is truly on our life, it becomes a gift to share with the world around us.

What we have come to call the Sermon on the Mount is a concise statement of Jesus' teachings on how to actually live in the reality of God's present kingdom available to us from the very space surrounding our bodies. It concludes with a statement that all who hear and do what he there says will have a life that can stand up to everything— that is, a life for eternity because it is already in the eternal (Matt. 7:24–25).

TALK ABOUT IT

When you look back over the past year, what is one thing that makes you say, "I'm blessed"?

Is it true that "Earth has no sorrow that heaven cannot heal?" It is true! That is precisely the gospel of heaven's availability that comes to us through the Beatitudes. And you don't have to wait until you're dead. Jesus offers to all such people as these the present blessedness of the present kingdom — regardless of circumstances. The condition of life sought for by human beings through the ages is attained in the quietly transforming friendship of Jesus.

VIDEO TEACHING NOTES

As you watch the video teaching segment for session two, featuring John Ortberg's conversation with Dallas Willard, use the following outline to record anything that stands out to you.

The most influential talk in human history

Three questions everyone needs to have answered — Question 1:
"What is real?"

Being safe in the kingdom of God

Question 2: "Who is well off (who is blessed)?"

Question 3: "How can I be a really good person?"

A fourth question: "How do I get to be a good person?"

The Beatitudes (blessed)

How the gospel becomes real

Jesus offers himself as God's doorway into the life that is truly life. Confidence in him leads us today, as in other times, to become his apprentices in eternal living. "Those who come through me will be safe," he said. "They will go in and out and find all they need. I have come into their world that they may have life, and life to the limit."

VIDEO DISCUSSION

1. Dallas Willard calls Jesus' Sermon on the Mount, with its dozens of famous passages, the most influential talk in human history. Scan Matthew 5–7 for a minute or two, then briefly share one big truth *you* have learned from the Sermon on the Mount and how it has impacted and shaped your life as a Christian.

2. **Read:** Matthew 4:17. What does Willard say Jesus is getting at when he declares, "Repent, for the kingdom of heaven is near"?

3. How does modern society define whether or not someone is well off, and how does Jesus' definition conflict with that?

4. What does Willard mean when he says that the world becomes a safe place when we are in God's kingdom?

5. **Read:** Romans 8:28, 37–39. What is the difference between saying, "All things are good," and saying, "All things work together for good"? Describe a time you experienced God taking something difficult, even bad, and working it out for good.

6. Some people try to navigate their way through life being well off (in the eyes of the world), but not being a really good person. Tell about a time you pursued such a path and how that turned out. What is one lesson you have learned about how to orient your life around God's kingdom instead of pursuing the enticements of this world?

The Beatitudes are not teachings on how to be blessed. They are not instructions to do anything. They do not indicate conditions that are especially pleasing to God or good for human beings.... They are explanations and illustrations, drawn from the immediate setting, of the present availability of the kingdom through personal relationship to Jesus. They single out cases that provide proof that, in him, the rule of God from the heavens truly is available in life circumstances that are beyond all human hope.

---

7. **Read:** Matthew 5:1 – 12. Where will the Beatitudes lead us if we understand them to be a list of things we are suppose to work at being?

How do the Beatitudes take on a whole new meaning if we see them as a declaration of who is welcome into the kingdom of God?

8. Willard gives a number of contemporary examples of who could be called blessed in our world today. Take a moment and write a short beatitude of your own:

Blessed are the ...

For as they walk in the presence of God's kingdom ...

Share your beatitude with the group and tell why this truth could bring such blessing to people.

9. What is one situation in your life where you need to expect and call for the presence of God and enter more into his kingdom life? How can your group members enter into this with you?

BONUS STUDY

If your group has time, you may choose to watch the bonus section of the video for session two now. (If not, consider viewing it on your own or as a group as part of your between-sessions activities.) Here are some reflection questions for the bonus section:

If there was a time when you believed the best pathway to spiritual formation was simply following the rules and obeying the Bible's teachings, where did this lead you in terms of spiritual growth?

According to Willard, what does it mean to "die to sin"? Why is this so difficult?

How does "living for Christ" and "walking in God's kingdom" make it possible to die to sin?

CLOSING PRAYER

Take time as a group to pray in some of the following directions:

- Pray for God to help you remember what is real and what matters most in life.
- Thank God that you are well off and pray that you will never forget who you are and what you have as a resident of God's kingdom and member of his family.
- Pray that when you get to the end of your life you will look back with confidence that you invested your heart, time, and resources in the things that matter most.
- Ask God to so fill you with an awareness of his blessing in your life that it will overflow to the people around you. (If you know a specific person who needs to experience God's blessing, pray that God will make you a conduit of his grace and love.)

You are really walking in the good news of the kingdom if you can go with confidence to any of the hopeless people around you and effortlessly convey assurance that they can now enter a blessed life with God.

BETWEEN SESSIONS

Personal Reflection

Dallas Willard and John Ortberg had a lively video conversation about the world being a safe place when we walk in the kingdom of God. Willard even gave a few examples of tough experiences that take on a whole new feel and tone when we see them through the lens of God's kingdom power and presence.

Take time to reflect on your own life. Where are some of the tough places you travel? In other words, what are some of the difficult things you face? How can your outlook be transformed if you see these things through eyes saturated in the realities of God's kingdom? What might you do to have a greater sense that the world is a perfectly safe place to be?

Personal Action

Willard says that the gospel becomes real when we can look at someone who is going through a hard time and let them know that they are blessed. Consider a person in your life who needs to hear this truth and what message of hope you might bring to them. During the next week, come alongside this person with words of blessing, actions of support, or provision of some kind. Pray that your presence will reflect and bring the kingdom of God right where they are, that God's blessing will flow through you and fill them.

Recommended Reading

In preparation for session three, you may want to read chapter 5 of the book *The Divine Conspiracy* by Dallas Willard.

JOURNAL, REFLECTIONS, AND NOTES

BECOMING A GOOD PERSON

The pathway to becoming a good person is not primarily about following a list of do's and don'ts but about a genuine love relationship with God and people.

INTRODUCTION

The only solid and lasting foundation for relationships is love. This includes our relationship with God as well as our relationships with others. Christians should be models of natural, genuine, and passionate love. Sadly, many in the world look at Christians and do not see us as good people who overflow with compassion and grace. Instead, they perceive us as being judgmental, harsh, and aloof from the needs of the world.

God wants his children to be good people. This means more than trying to act good. God actually wants to transform each of us from the inside out. Goodness does not come from following a checklist of religious "do's" and "don'ts." It is so much bigger than that. Goodness grows in our hearts and lives when we authentically care about God, others, and even ourselves and express that love freely.

Throughout the journey of life a gap will always exist between who we are and what God wants us to be. This is why God is patient with us and why we need to be patient with ourselves. We ought not get discouraged or frustrated with our shortcomings. In such moments we simply receive grace and invite God's Spirit to continue the transformation process. God is teaching us and shaping us into good people, but this process will take a lifetime.

No good tree produces bad fruit, nor any bad tree good fruit.... The good person, from the good treasured up in his heart, produces what is good.

LUKE 6:43–45 (AUTHOR PARAPHRASE)

TALK ABOUT IT

Tell about a time you watched a little child express love to a parent or sibling spontaneously and freely. How are such moments a model of what God wants from and for all of his children?

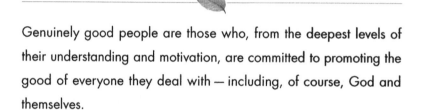

Genuinely good people are those who, from the deepest levels of their understanding and motivation, are committed to promoting the good of everyone they deal with — including, of course, God and themselves.

VIDEO TEACHING NOTES

As you watch the video teaching segment for session three, featuring John Ortberg's conversation with Dallas Willard, use the following outline to record anything that stands out to you.

Who is a good person ... according to Jesus?

True love is . . .

A good person genuinely cares for those around them

Caring for yourself

A good person lives in a genuine love relationship with God

Blessing and cursing

Why should I want to become a good person?

The inability to be insulted

If I am not immersed in the reality of this kingdom of life, it will not seem good or right to me to forgo reputation, pride, vanity, and wealth, and I will inescapably be driven to pursue them.

VIDEO DISCUSSION

1. "Love is the basis, the foundation, of all human relationships." How have you seen relationships thrive when there is a free flow of love and how have you seen them wither when love is withheld?

2. **Read:** 2 Corinthians 1:3–7. John Ortberg tells the story about his daughter Laura comforting herself with her mother's words when she would wake up in the middle of the night. In your times of stress, pain, loss, and fear, what words from your heavenly Father might you speak to yourself that would bring peace and hope?

3. Dallas Willard and John Ortberg talk about how many people do not have positive and love-filled images come to mind when they think of Christians. What are some of the perceptions people in your community have of Christians (both good and bad), and what has created these pictures in their minds?

4. What will the Christian faith look like if our primary driving force is what we do (or refrain from doing), in other words, how we perform for God? How will our faith look different if it is based on who we are in Christ and what we are becoming as we grow in our relationship with him?

5. **Read:** 1 John 3:16–19. What are signs and indicators that we are genuinely caring for the people around us?

6. One person we should care for is ourself. As a matter of fact, if we don't genuinely care for ourselves, it can be very difficult to care for others around us. Respond to *one* of the following questions:

- What are things we can do to care for ourselves?

- How does this self-care honor God?

- What is one way you personally need to take more time and energy to care for yourself?

7. **Read:** Luke 6:27–31. Willard says, "Most of us have ample opportunity to bless those who curse us." Tell about a time you were cursed in some way and how you responded. How might it look when we learn to bless those who curse us?

Jesus tells us to love our enemies and to carry that love through with the highest act of love, prayer. "Love your enemies and pray for those persecuting you. In this way you take on the nature of your Father, the one in the heavens, who routinely gives good things, such as sunshine and rain, to both the evil and the good, to those who are godly and those who spit in his face" (Matt. 5:44–45).

8. How might *one* of the following activities or behaviors be transformed if we asked ourselves, "How would I be doing this if I was doing it as an act of love?" rather than simply as a duty or for the approval of others?

   • Doing housework

   • Volunteering at church or a nonprofit ministry

   • Mowing a neighbor's lawn while they are out of town

   • Spending time with your child or a friend

   • Working a full day at your place of employment

   • Other _____

9. As we become more and more like Jesus and love the way he did, pride, fear, domination, and other negative attitudes have less impact on our

relationships. Tell about how you have seen a negative attitude that used to mark your relationships begin to dissipate because of your growing relationship with Jesus.

What is a negative attitude or pattern with which you still struggle, and how might your group members pray for you and support you as you seek for transformation to take place?

10. Who is a person in your life that makes you say, "I want to be good like them"? What about their life so attracts you?

A good person is one who genuinely cares for those around them, the people whose life they affect just by being there.

BONUS STUDY

If your group has time, you may choose to watch the bonus section of the video for session three now. (If not, consider viewing it on your own or as a group as part of your between-sessions activities.) Here are some reflection questions for the bonus section:

Willard writes, "Spirituality wrongly understood or pursued is a major source of human misery and rebellion against God." What is he getting at with this statement, and how have you seen this reality in the lives of "religious" people?

Some people try to base their righteousness on what they "don't do." What are some things people try to refrain from when they are working at being righteous? Why is following a "don't do" list a dead-end in terms of true righteousness?

CLOSING PRAYER

Take time as a group to pray in some of the following directions:

- Thank God for his love in your life and how it allows you to love others.
- Pray for the comfort and grace of God to overflow in the lives of people you know who are struggling today.
- Ask God to correct any images or pictures you have of him that are faulty and unhealthy.
- Pray that your relationship with God and life of faith will give others an accurate and positive picture of Christians.
- If there are ways you are not caring for yourself, pray that God will reveal them and help you take action to do wise and Christ-honoring self-care.

Doing and not just hearing and talking about it is how we know the reality of the kingdom and integrate our life into it.

BETWEEN SESSIONS

Personal Reflection

Willard makes these statements: "Love is the opposite of rejection" and "Acceptance is an empty term." What does he mean and what does this say to a culture that talks a lot about "acceptance" and not enough about "love"? Where are you driven by a desire for acceptance and what can you do to move toward being more motivated by love?

Personal Action

Our lives and relationships grow healthier when we understand that people's compliments don't make us a better person and their criticisms don't make us a bad person. Think about how your life might change if you walked through each day aware that you don't answer to other people but only to God.

During the coming week identify when you are driven by a desire to gain the approval of people. Also, take note when the disapproval of people discourages you or makes you feel bad about yourself. In these moments, pause to pray. Ask God to help you remember that his approval and affirmation are all you need. Pray for freedom from being manipulated or controlled by the need for approval or fear of disapproval.

Recommended Reading

In preparation for session four, you may want to read chapter 6 of the book *The Divine Conspiracy* by Dallas Willard.

JOURNAL, REFLECTIONS, AND NOTES

TREASURING WHAT MATTERS MOST

We can treasure God, or we can treasure the stuff of this world. Jesus invites us to make a decision, each and every day, to treasure what matters most!

INTRODUCTION

God is radiant, lovable, happy, accessible, and closer than we think. He is worthy of being our greatest treasure. But all kinds of counterfeits constantly cry for our attention and invite our allegiance. Each day of our life we can make a decision to hold God as the treasure of our heart.

Through Jesus Christ we have been reconciled to the Father and have unfettered access to this life-giving relationship. Because of Jesus' life, death, resurrection, and ascension, ordinary people like you and me can come near to God without fear and enter a whole new kind of life. This kingdom living is not reserved for a future date when this life ends. It is here and now.

As we learn to walk in this new reality, we discover that the things we treasure begin to change. The pursuit of money, the need for power, and the passion for pleasure begin to pale compared to the treasure of knowing God, loving people, and walking in the kingdom. Our compulsion to manage our appearances and impress people gives way to an authentic desire to please our loving heavenly Father.

How can you have faith when you seek glory from one another and do not seek the glory that comes from the one who alone is God?

JOHN 5:44 (AUTHOR PARAPHRASE)

TALK ABOUT IT

If you interviewed people on the street and asked them this simple question, "What do you treasure most in this world?" what common answers might you get? If you followed those same people around with a video camera for a week, capturing all they said and did, what might these images teach you about what they actually treasure most?

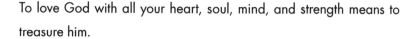

To love God with all your heart, soul, mind, and strength means to treasure him.

VIDEO TEACHING NOTES

As you watch the video teaching segment for session four, featuring John Ortberg's conversation with Dallas Willard, use the following outline to record anything that stands out to you.

Our God of love

Wrong pictures of God

God as creator and ruler of the universe, and God as shepherd

Our need to treasure things

A life-giving perspective on money

Managing appearances

Giving and prayer

The goodness of God

If we live unto God alone, he responds to our expectations — which are of him alone.... Live as if the only one whose opinion mattered were God.

VIDEO DISCUSSION

1. Dallas Willard writes, "The acid test for any theology is this: Is the God presented one that can be loved, heart, soul, mind and strength? If the thoughtful, honest answer is, 'Not really!' then we need to look elsewhere or deeper." How does a vision of a loving, accessible, competent God mesh with the way most people perceive God today?

   How do you respond to this picture of God?

2. **Read:** John 14:8 – 11. What is Jesus teaching Philip and the rest of his followers about the Father? What implications does this have on those who want to paint a picture of God the Father that is dramatically different than the picture of Jesus Christ given to us in the Gospels?

3. Some people feel fearful and intimidated by God. Like Dorothy in the movie *The Wizard of Oz*, they tremble and want to run away in the presence of the "great and powerful Oz." Is this feeling of fear and intimidation legitimate and helpful, or inappropriate and damaging to our faith? Explain.

4. **Read:** Romans 5:9–11; 2 Corinthians 5:17–21; and Colossians 1:21–23. How do the pictures in these passages help define and deepen our understanding of how we can relate with God the Father?

5. Willard talks about the human need to organize itself around valued things. Take a moment to write down four or five things you value.

    * _____
    * _____
    * _____
    * _____
    * _____

    What is it about these things that you value and how would you feel if you lost them?

Everyone has treasures. This is an essential part of what it is to be human. To have nothing that one treasures is to be in a nonhuman condition.

6. Respond to this statement: "What we value determines our identity." What are things we should value in order that we might become more the people God desires us to be?

7. **Read:** Matthew 6:19–24. Willard says, "If you treasure money, it will throw your whole life out of kilter." Identify some of the warning signs that we are treasuring money. How might we respond when we see these signs popping up in our lives?

8. **Read:** 1 John 2:15–17. Managing appearances (maintaining facades) just might be the single most obsessive preoccupation of human beings. Give some examples of how Satan uses the "lust of the eyes"—as in the desire to "look good"—to tempt people today.

What can we do to identify and resist these temptations when they confront us?

Whatever our position in life, if our lives and works are to be of the kingdom of God, we must not have human approval as a primary or even major aim. We must lovingly allow people to think whatever they will.

---

9. **Read:** Matthew 6:1 – 8, 16 – 18. What is Jesus getting at when he teaches us about praying, giving, and fasting "in secret"? How can flaunting these spiritual disciplines and practices become a matter of "appearance management"?

Some have taken the idea of doing these things "in secret" to mean that we should never talk about these areas of our spiritual lives. How might this be missing the point?

The person who gives without regard to who is looking and does not even notice it as anything special themselves, no "big deal," is the very one who has God's attention and becomes God's creative partner in well-doing.... Characteristically, people like this are well known for how much they can accomplish. But we should know, as Jesus knew, that it is because of "the hand of God" engaged along with them.

BONUS STUDY

If your group has time, you may choose to watch the bonus section of the video for session four now. (If not, consider viewing it on your own or as a group as part of your between-sessions activities.) Here are some reflection questions for the bonus section:

What are some real-life situations where kids tend to ask, "How did I do?" Why do they ask this question ... what are they looking for?

What are some settings and situations where adults still wonder, "How did I do?" Why do we still need this affirmation as adults?

Read: 2 Corinthians 10:10. Paul lived with unfair criticism and so will we. What are some practical ways you have learned to look past the comments and critique of others? What can we do to keep our focus on what God thinks about us?

How do you respond to the idea of "laughing at the devil"? How can this be a good strategy? Why might it be wise to be careful how far we take this?

CLOSING PRAYER

Take time as a group to pray in some of the following directions:

- Thank God for being worthy of love and praise, of being treasured.
- Pray for eyes to see where you are treasuring things that are not of true and lasting value.
- Ask God to help you shift your attention and heart away from false treasures.
- Confess ways you spend time in "appearance management" and pray for the power you need to be authentic before God and people.

One is blessed if one's life is based upon acceptance and intimate interactions with what God is doing in human history. Such people are in the present kingdom of the heavens.

BETWEEN SESSIONS

Personal Reflection

When money gets its grip on you and becomes a treasure, how does this impact your life—your relationships with God, family, and friends; service to others; etc.? If the stuff of this world has a wrongful place in your life right now, what steps can you take to diminish its influence and increase your love for God?

Personal Action

In the coming week read Psalm 23 and the Lord's Prayer (Matthew 6:9–13) several times each. As you read these brief but powerful passages, reflect on God's provision, his love, and how you can treasure him more fully. Then, sit down and write a personal note of thanks and praise to God for all he has done for you in the past and all he is doing today!

Recommended Reading

In preparation for session five, you may want to read chapter 7 of the book *The Divine Conspiracy* by Dallas Willard.

JOURNAL, REFLECTIONS, AND NOTES

BECOMING A COMMUNITY
OF PRAYERFUL LOVE

The Lord's Prayer is more than a recitation of certain words and requests. It is an invitation to talk with God, throughout our day, about the things we are doing together.

INTRODUCTION

God is building a community of prayerful love right here on the earth. As his kingdom breaks into our daily lives, we discover that prayer is so much more than we ever dreamed.

Prayer is far more than memorizing a set of words or statements and repeating them back to the sky, hoping God will hear.

Prayer is much deeper than blocking out a time in the morning or evening and giving God a wish list of the things we hope he will do.

Prayer is certainly more dynamic than calling out to God but refusing to actually take action that will help fulfill his will for our lives and the world.

What we need for kingdom living is a *praying life*, not just a prayer life.

In the Lord's Prayer Jesus mentions a number of topics we can talk with God about. These are not the only topics, but they are a great starting place! This beautiful prayer becomes a natural conversation starter for us and the one who is building a community of love on the earth, our Father.

The picture of prayer that emerges from the life and teaching of Jesus in the Gospels is quite clear. Basically it is one of asking, requesting things from God.

TALK ABOUT IT

If you grew up being taught to pray, describe the typical form and content of prayer you learned. Did your style of childhood prayers help you learn authentic prayer, or did it get in the way of you really learning about prayer? Explain.

Prayer, it is rightly said, is the method of genuine theological research, the method of understanding what and who God is. God is spirit and exists at the level of reality where the human heart, or spirit, also exists, serving as the foundation and source of our visible life. It is there that the individual meets with God "in spirit and in truth."

In kingdom life we extend the respect to others that we would naturally hope others would extend to us. That is how love behaves, and it still behaves that way when we come to our intimate relationships.

VIDEO TEACHING NOTES

As you watch the video teaching segment for session five, featuring John Ortberg's conversation with Dallas Willard, use the following outline to record anything that stands out to you.

A community of prayerful love

Understanding the idea of "kingdom"

"Don't judge" ... but what does that mean?

Condemnation engineering

The "Lord's Prayer"

    The address

    Areas of request

Prayer is talking to God about things we're doing together

Integrating life and prayer

How beautiful it is to see relationships in which asking and receiving are a joyful and loving way of life. Often we see those who cherish one another each seriously or playfully trying to outgive the other. That is how relationships should be.

VIDEO DISCUSSION

1. How does Dallas Willard define kingdom in terms of "my kingdom" and "God's kingdom"? How do these definitions bring fresh understanding of the word "kingdom"?

2. **Read:** Matthew 7:7–12 and Matthew 6:9–13. Willard says, "Some people do *not* think asking is the proper attitude in prayer." How does Jesus feel about us asking things of God? What are examples of how "asking" can become unhealthy and out of control?

3. **Read:** Matthew 7:1–5. What is Jesus getting at when he tells us not to judge others?

   Share examples of how we try to manage people by condemning them. Why is this a dangerous and hurtful practice?

4. **Read:** Matthew 7:6. What is Jesus getting at when he talks about giving "dogs what is sacred"?

   What does Willard mean by "condemnation engineering" and how have you seen Christians do this with each other?

The problem with pearls for pigs is not that the pigs are not worthy. It is not worthiness that is in question here at all, but helpfulness. Pigs cannot digest pearls, cannot nourish themselves upon them.

---

5. **Read again:** Matthew 6:9–13. Jesus invites us to address God as "Father," which Willard says strips away religious jargon and makes God accessible. If we could learn to see God as a loving, providing, protecting, and tender Father, how might this impact the way we pray?

6. Willard offers some very unique ways to understand the specific content of the Lord's Prayer. How does he explain the meaning of "in heaven," and how is this a fresh new perspective on these words?

7. **Read:** Matthew 6:9 and Exodus 20:3. How do the first commandment and the invitation to pray "Hallowed be your name" work together to help us keep a healthy perspective on *who* is valuable and *what* is good?

Only a vivid assurance of God's greatness and goodness can lay a foundation for the life of prayer, and such an assurance will certainly express itself in praise.

8. **Read:** 1 Thessalonians 5:17. One simple definition of prayer is: "talking to God about things we're doing together." How does this definition fit with your understanding of prayer, and how might your prayer life be changed or deepened if you adopted it?

9. In John Ortberg and Dallas Willard's brief but important interchange about the relationship of planning (taking action) and praying, they admit that some people see planning as contrary to dependence on God. Name some times that planning and taking action are very important in the life of a Christian. In these moments, how do planning and praying actually fit well together?

Prayer is at home in ordinary life.

BONUS STUDY

If your group has time, you may choose to watch the bonus section of the video for session five now. (If not, consider viewing it on your own or as a group as part of your between-sessions activities.) Here are some reflection questions for the bonus section:

Willard says, "Asking is a kind of cosmic power." How have you experienced the power of asking in human relationships? How have you seen the power of asking in your relationship with God?

Describe an occasion when you simply made eye contact with a person and surprising data was communicated. How can a person make a request or communicate with their face?

Read: Numbers 6:22–27. What are we asking when we pray for God to "make his face shine" on someone? What does it mean for God to "turn his face toward" someone? Why is this a great prayer of blessing?

Tell about a time when you had a real sense that God was turning his face toward you, looking at you, and taking delight in you. How did this make you feel?

CLOSING PRAYER

Many people in various church traditions have a practice of reading the Lord's Prayer together in unison. In his book, *The Divine Conspiracy*, Dallas writes his own paraphrase of the Lord's Prayer. Pause as a group to read this version together (slowly and reflectively):

> Dear Father always near us,
> may your name be treasured and loved,
> may your rule be completed in us —
> may your will be done here on earth
> in just the way it is done in heaven.
> Give us today the things we need today,
> and forgive us our sins and impositions on you,
> as we are forgiving all who in any way offend us.
> Please don't put us through trials,
> but deliver us from everything bad.
> Because you are the one in charge,
> And you have all the power,
> And the glory too is all yours — forever —
> which is just the way we want it.
> Amen (or, Whoopie)!

Talk together about one new lesson you have learned from this study of the Lord's Prayer and how it might influence the way you pray and live.

BETWEEN SESSIONS

Personal Reflection

Dallas Willard and John Ortberg believe that planning and praying should go hand in hand, and not be seen as opposing activities. As you walk through your day, take note of where you tend to pray but avoid action. Also, look for times when you are prone to take action but don't talk to God about what you are doing. Make a point of seeking to bring your prayers and action together. Add prayer to your moments of action. Add action to your times of prayer.

Personal Action

During the coming week read and pray through the Lord's Prayer each day. Don't simply recite it. Use it as a springboard into conversation with God. When you pray, "Give us today our daily bread," talk with God about the simple needs of life and ask him to take care of you. When you pray about God not leading you into temptation, tell him about the things you will face today that may tempt you or be a trial to you and ask for his power to overcome. Let this conversation linger and continue through the whole day.

Recommended Reading

In preparation for session six, you may want to read chapters 8 – 10 of the book *The Divine Conspiracy* by Dallas Willard.

JOURNAL, REFLECTIONS, AND NOTES

LIVING AS A DISCIPLE OF JESUS

Being a disciple is not about mastering specific activities or disciplines, it is about becoming an apprentice of the Savior and letting his continual presence shape, inform, and impact everything we do, and all we are becoming.

INTRODUCTION

Two thousand years ago Jesus walked the landscape of Palestine and invited people to become his disciples. As each person enrolled in the school of Jesus, they became his apprentice. Simply put, this meant they spent time with the Savior, learned from him, followed his teachings, and became more and more like their leader, Jesus.

Things have not changed all that much since then. Jesus still calls people to follow him and the goal is the same—life transformation.

Today many people have a confused understanding of what it means to be a disciple. They think in terms of exercising certain disciplines, engaging in particular actions, and refraining from some "off-limits" behaviors. This is not the heart of Jesus or the vision of discipleship. Being a disciple is about becoming like Jesus, our Master and Maestro.

God is not looking for us to earn his favor and love. He already offers these things freely ... by grace. What Jesus calls us to do is to abide. We are to stay close to him, follow his ways, and emulate his life. As we do this, the plan of God unfolds right where we are. Heaven breaks into ordinary life and the kingdom is near.

Who teaches you? Whose disciple are you? One thing is sure: You are somebody's disciple. You learned how to live from somebody else. There are no exceptions to this rule.

TALK ABOUT IT

Tell about when you felt or heard Jesus' invitation to become his student. How did this invitation come, and what is one way it has changed the trajectory of your life?

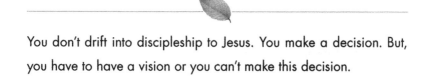

You don't drift into discipleship to Jesus. You make a decision. But, you have to have a vision or you can't make this decision.

VIDEO TEACHING NOTES

As you watch the video teaching segment for session six, featuring John Ortberg's conversation with Dallas Willard, use the following outline to record anything that stands out to you.

The call of Jesus for people to become his students

What does it look like when a person lives as a disciple of Jesus?

Hearing about Jesus and knowing something about the kingdom of God

Understanding that the kingdom of God is right here, right now!

The critical place of obedience

The place of spiritual disciplines

Grace, effort, and earning

VIDEO DISCUSSION

1. **Read:** Colossians 2:2–3. Dallas Willard remarks that Jesus is Lord but he is also "a really smart guy!" What is one teaching of Jesus in the Gospels, or a story about Jesus, that reveals his great wisdom?

2. When a pastor or church leader says, "You should be a disciple of Jesus," or, "You need to grow as a disciple of Jesus," what are some of the activities or traits they are usually talking about? As a group, make a list in the space provided below and on page 82:

   A disciple of Jesus ...

   A disciple of Jesus ...

   A disciple of Jesus ...

   A disciple of Jesus ...

A disciple of Jesus . . .

A disciple of Jesus . . .

How can these things help you grow as a disciple? How are they not the whole story when it comes to discipleship?

I can't assume my spiritual life is going well just because I am practicing a lot of disciplines. When I am tempted to make this the measure of how I am doing, I remind myself that the Pharisees were known for using this standard.

---

3. Willard says that to be a follower of Jesus (to be his apprentice) we have to know some things about Jesus and his kingdom. What are some of the things that are important for a person to know about Jesus and his kingdom to truly be his disciple?

4. Knowing the kingdom of God is right here, right now means that we do everything with a sense that God is near and active in our lives. Identify some areas of life in which it is easy to forget that God is with us. What can we do to notice God's presence more in these places and situations?

5. Willard says, "The next time you are tempted to do what you know to be wrong, do your best to do what is right and expect God to bail you out!" What is one situation you might face in the coming month where you will have an opportunity to try doing what you know is right—even if this action or decision stretches you?

6. Respond to this statement: "Spiritual disciplines are not an issue of righteousness, but an issue of wisdom." Why is it wise to develop spiritual disciplines in our daily life?

When I am going to evaluate my spiritual condition, I don't ask, "How am I doing with spiritual disciplines?" Instead, I ask, "Am I easily irritated?" This is often a better measuring stick.

7. "Grace is not opposed to effort," says Willard, "it is opposed to earning." How does God, in his grace, celebrate our effort? Why is grace in opposition to our sense that we need to earn God's love and favor?

8. **Read:** James 1:22–25. We need to understand that abiding in God's Word is not about entering a nonstop regimen of Bible study. It is about putting what we learn from the Word into practice in ordinary life. What keeps us from applying and living what we learn from the teaching of Jesus?

9. **Read:** Numbers 6:22–27. A benediction is speaking blessing on a person. Consider someone in your life who needs a word of blessing. What might you say to them that will impart the grace and blessing of God?

BONUS STUDY

If your group has time, you may choose to watch the bonus section of the video for session six now. (If not, consider viewing it on your own or as a group in the coming days.) Here are some reflection questions for the bonus section:

After listening to Dallas Willard and John Ortberg define and describe "spiritual disciplines," what new insight do you have to the value of developing the disciplines in your life?

Tell about an area of your life where you have developed a process of exercising discipline (learning an instrument, playing a sport, studying a language, etc.). How did discipline help you succeed? How was discipline a good thing?

What is one spiritual discipline you have found to be difficult, and how might you develop a program to grow this discipline in your spiritual life, even though it stretches you?

You don't get more faith by trying harder. You get faith as a gift from your experience of God and that comes in your real world.

CLOSING PRAYER

Take time as a group to pray in some of the following directions:

- Jesus was a "really smart guy!" Pray that you will grow in wisdom and use your mind to glorify God.
- Thank God for inviting you to be his disciple. Let him know you feel honored and privileged to spend your life growing as his apprentice.
- Ask God to help you grow in the spiritual disciplines, but pray that these will simply be a way to become more like Jesus. Pray that they will never become a source of spiritual pride or self-righteousness.
- Pray for opportunities to bring benediction (words of blessing) to those you encounter each day.

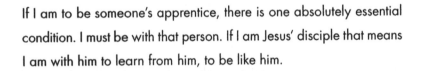

If I am to be someone's apprentice, there is one absolutely essential condition. I must be with that person. If I am Jesus' disciple that means I am with him to learn from him, to be like him.

IN THE COMING DAYS

Personal Reflection

Dallas Willard and John Ortberg talked at length about the idea that spiritual practices are not an end in themselves, but are meant to connect us to Jesus, teach us wisdom, and eventually help transform our lives. Spend some time thinking about how you have engaged in the spiritual disciplines and what has resulted from doing so. Have they led to transformation? Have they made you more obedient to Jesus? Have they unleashed the presence of God's kingdom in your daily life, your home, and your community?

Personal Action

Willard wrote a wonderful book called *The Spirit of the Disciplines* (Harper-One, 1990), which goes into greater depth on the various disciplines and the condition of our heart as we seek to grow as disciples. You might want to read this book as a follow-up to this small group study.

Recommended Reading

As further follow-up, you may also want to reread Willard's *The Divine Conspiracy* (or any portion of the book you were unable to finish during the study).

JOURNAL, REFLECTIONS, AND NOTES

Be sure to explore these other titles by Dallas Willard:

Share Your Thoughts

With the Author: Your comments will be forwarded to
the author when you send them to *zauthor@zondervan.com*.

With Zondervan: Submit your review of this book
by writing to *zreview@zondervan.com*.

Free Online Resources at
www.zondervan.com

Zondervan AuthorTracker: Be notified whenever your favorite
authors publish new books, go on tour, or post an update
about what's happening in their lives at www.zondervan.com/
authortracker.

Daily Bible Verses and Devotions: Enrich your life with daily
Bible verses or devotions that help you start every morning
focused on God. Visit www.zondervan.com/newsletters.

Free Email Publications: Sign up for newsletters on Christian
living, academic resources, church ministry, fiction, children's
resources, and more. Visit www.zondervan.com/newsletters.

Zondervan Bible Search: Find and compare Bible passages in
a variety of translations at www.zondervanbiblesearch.com.

Other Benefits: Register yourself to receive online benefits
like coupons and special offers, or to participate in research.